BUILDING A
DREAM

MARY BETHUNE'S SCHOOL

By Richard Kelso
Illustrations by Debbe Heller

METRO NONFICTION BOOKBAG

METROPOLITAN TEACHING AND LEARNING COMPANY

Cover Illustration by Antonio Wade

Metropolitan Teaching and Learning Company
33 Irving Place
New York, NY 10003
ISBN: 1-58830-201-6

1 2 3 4 5 6 7 8 9 LB 04 03 02 01

Dedication

Alex Haley was General Editor of the first books in the Metro Nonfiction Bookbag. In this role, he provided editorial direction through all stages of book development, and wrote a special introduction for each selection.

Those of us who carried on with the project after Mr. Haley's death did our best to reflect his spirit in the stories. We hope that readers will find evidence of Alex Haley's influence on these pages, just as we felt his influence while completing them.

The books in the Metro Nonfiction Bookbag are Alex Haley's contribution to the education of America's young people. This book is respectfully dedicated to his memory.

Introduction
by Alex Haley, General Editor

Nowadays, if you are of school age, going to school is the most ordinary thing in the world. But it wasn't always so. For many Americans in the early 1900s, school was at best a dream. If you were poor, female, and black, it was something else as well. It was impossible.

But some people dreamed anyway. Mary McLeod Bethune, who was poor, female, and black, was one who followed her dream. And she shared it with others. This is her story.

Dreamers like Mrs. Bethune give us more than just what they have accomplished. They give us their example. By their example they teach us that dreaming is the first step in doing the impossible. So if you have a dream, live it. Make the impossible happen.

To my Grandmother,
Joburness Hazel Redmon Kelso

Contents

1

A Chance to Learn

The train let out a long, loud whistle as it chugged into Daytona Beach, Florida. A few black boys and girls were playing on the dusty ground near the tracks. As the train came nearer, they scattered, waving at the passengers as they ran away.

From one of the coach windows, Mrs. Mary McLeod Bethune and her four-year-old son, Albert, waved back. She was glad to see the children, but she was worried about them, too. She thought they should be in school, learning to read and write. Mrs. Bethune believed children should learn skills

1

that would help them to get good jobs when they were old enough. That is just why she had come to Daytona Beach on this warm September day in 1904.

Mrs. Bethune was a young teacher. She knew that in most southern towns in 1904 there were separate schools for black children and white children. At the time, it was against the law for children of both races to go to the same school. Some towns had schools for whites but none for blacks, so black children in those towns could not go to school at all. This made Mrs. Bethune angry. It also made her determined to do something about it. She wanted more schools for black children, and she wanted them to be good schools.

When Mrs. Bethune was a young girl, she had been just like the children she had seen playing outside the train window moments before. She had not been able to start school until she was eleven years old. None of her fourteen older brothers and sisters had gone to school at all. There had been no schools for black children in their hometown of Mayesville, South Carolina, when they were growing up.

• • •

But that had changed. Mrs. Bethune had been lucky. She could still remember the day when she first heard that she would be going to school. That day her parents, Mr. and Mrs. McLeod, came home from town with exciting news. A school for black children had opened just five miles away! A huge smile swept across her face as she listened. Attending school would be a dream come true. But first her parents had to decide if they could do without Mary's help on the family farm.

They gave the matter some thought and then decided that, as the youngest, Mary could probably be spared from farmwork long enough to attend school. But she would have to make time to do her chores. And she would have to walk to school. No one could be spared to take her back and forth every day.

So each weekday for six years, young Mary McLeod had gladly walked five long miles down a dirt country road to the one-room schoolhouse.

At school Mary learned very fast, and when she came home, she would share what she had learned with her family and neighbors. Soon grown-ups all over Mayesville—both black and white—were asking her to read letters they could not read. She helped them figure out the weight of the cotton they grew and how much it was worth. And she helped them calculate how much money they owed at the general store.

Then Mary won a scholarship to a school in North Carolina that trained new teachers. Everyone in Mayesville turned out to say goodbye to Mary when the time came for her to leave home. They were proud of her. She had helped them, so they wanted to help her. Some made clothes for her. Some prepared food for the long trip. And they all wished her well.

Mary studied hard in North Carolina. She read many books about many subjects. She learned as much as she could about the world. She also gained knowledge about farming, sewing, running a household, helping sick people, and raising and teaching children. When she was ready to share her knowledge with others, Mary became a teacher.

Her first teaching job was at the school she had gone to as a girl in Mayesville. Then she moved to Augusta, Georgia, to help another teacher, Miss Lucy Laney, who had a school for black girls. Miss Laney's school gave Mary the idea of starting her own school.

After a year at Miss Laney's school, Mary met and married Albertus Bethune, another teacher. The Bethunes moved to Palatka, Florida, where Mrs. Bethune taught for two years at a church school. But the idea of Miss

Laney's school kept tugging at Mrs. Bethune's mind. She began looking around for a place to start her own school.

Mrs. Bethune learned that many black workers had been hired to work on the railroad being built along Florida's east coast. Much of the work was being done around Daytona Beach. Mrs. Bethune knew that the workers would bring their families with them, and she knew their children would need a school. Daytona Beach seemed just the place to start a school. Seeing the children playing along the tracks as her train came into town, she knew she had made the right choice.

● ● ●

But Mrs. Bethune had never started her own school before. Where would she find a building to use as a school? Where would she get desks, chairs, and other things the school needed? Would any parents send their children to her school?

Many questions passed through her mind

as the train came to a stop. But she was sure that she would find a way to build her school. It was her dream, and she would make it come true.

2

An Old Cabin Near the Dump

Mrs. Bethune knocked on the door of a small wooden house in Daytona's black neighborhood. Three girls opened the door together and giggled with surprise to see the woman and her son at their door. The girls were Lena, Lucille, and Ruth Warren.

In a moment Mrs. Warren herself came to the door. She had not been expecting any visitors, so she greeted Mrs. Bethune with a warm but puzzled look. Then Mrs. Bethune introduced herself. She explained that Reverend Pratt in Palatka, Florida, had given her Mrs. Warren's name. "I am going to open a school for Negro girls," Mrs. Bethune said. Reverend Pratt had told her that she might be able to stay with Mrs. Warren until she got her school started.

Mrs. Warren's puzzled look changed to a broad, welcoming smile when she heard her friend Reverend Pratt's name. She invited Mrs. Bethune inside, and they began to talk. In no time, everything was settled. Mrs. Warren's daughters agreed to give up their room so that Mrs. Bethune and Albert could sleep there.

Mrs. Bethune was grateful, and tired from her train trip, but she couldn't think about sleeping just then. She had work to do. She told Mrs. Warren she needed to find a building that she could turn into a school. "Do you know of anybody who would rent me a place?" she asked.

Mrs. Warren thought a moment. Then she said she believed Mr. Williams, the carpenter, had an old cabin for rent on Palm Street, down by the dump. Mrs. Bethune decided to go see him right away.

On her way to Mr. Williams's cabin, Mrs. Bethune noticed how different the black neighborhood was from the white neighborhood. In the black neighborhood, the roads were not paved. They were muddy and full of deep ruts. There were no sidewalks or lampposts. These were things the city government should have taken care of but didn't because the people were black and poor.

Here and there Mrs. Bethune saw a neat, nicely painted house. But most of the houses were run-down shacks with no running water.

The white neighborhoods of Daytona Beach had big, fine houses and elegant hotels. The paved streets were lit at night by gas lamps. Mrs. Bethune hoped that one day her people would have fine homes and neighborhoods, too. The government would not help blacks the way it helped whites. Black people would have to do it themselves. But they needed good jobs. For good jobs, Mrs. Bethune knew, they would need good schools. Her goal was to start a school

11

so that her people could someday live in a better way.

She continued on her way and found Mr. Williams sitting on the porch of a shabby old cabin.

"Hello," she called out. "I'm Mrs. Bethune." She said Mrs. Warren told her he might have a cabin to rent. Mrs. Bethune asked how much it would cost to rent the place.

"I can rent it to you for eleven dollars a month," Mr. Williams said.

Mrs. Bethune looked in her purse. She really didn't need to; she knew exactly how much money she had. She had a dollar fifty and not a penny more. But she didn't want Mr. Williams to know how little she had. After fussing in her purse for a bit, she presented five dimes to Mr. Williams.

"Thank you, sir," she said. This money, she explained with a smile, was her down payment on the cabin rent. She told Mr. Williams he would have the remaining ten dollars and fifty cents by the end of the month.

Mr. Williams opened his mouth to speak. He wasn't done bargaining! But before he could say a word, Mrs. Bethune opened the door and went inside the cabin. She and Mr. Williams had made a deal. As far as she was concerned, the cabin was hers.

Now it was time to see what kind of work it needed. She could see that the whole place needed to be painted. She counted four rooms downstairs and three upstairs. There was a fireplace, but she would need to get a stove, too. The windows seemed to be in pretty good shape. There was dust everywhere, of course, and cobwebs. But she was excited and sure that she could quickly fix up the cabin.

She came back onto the porch and looked down at the broken boards in the steps. Those would need to be mended, too. Then, without waiting, she said good day to Mr. Williams and hurried off.

Mrs. Bethune had her cabin, but there was much work to be done before it would be a school. Mrs. Bethune didn't worry. She believed in herself. She believed in her dream. She believed in her people. And she believed in God. She knew she would find a way.

Mrs. Bethune didn't waste any time. She began visiting houses in the neighborhood to tell people about her school. She went to churches on Sunday and talked to people there. If there was a door, she knocked on it. If she saw two people standing by the side of the road, she would go up to them. She was not shy.

"My school," she told people, "will begin as a school for girls." She felt that girls needed more help than boys in order to get good jobs. Boys learned skills around the farm that would help them get farmwork or jobs as laborers—like building the railroad. They weren't great jobs, but they paid better than the kinds of jobs girls could get without education or special training.

"This is a new kind of school," she said. "I

am going to teach my girls crafts and home-making. I am going to teach them to earn a living. They will be trained in head, hand, and heart. Their heads to think, their hands to work, and their hearts to have faith." People listened to Mrs. Bethune. They liked what she told them.

Most of the people Mrs. Bethune talked to had little or no money, but when she asked, they helped. They gave food from their kitchens and gardens. They sold fish dinners and chicken dinners and gave the money to Mrs. Bethune to help build the school.

When Mrs. Bethune met people with children, she asked them to send their children to her school. She was charging just fifty cents a week. If they couldn't afford the fifty cents, she told them to send their girls anyway. She was sure she'd find a way to meet expenses.

She went around to the white neighborhoods, too. She rang doorbells and talked to anyone who would listen. She went to white churches, clubs, and lodges. Everywhere she went she asked for money, food, old furniture, clothing—anything that would help her school. Some people offered help, but others refused to even listen to her. Some were rude. But Mrs. Bethune was always polite. "Thank you for your time," she'd say as she calmly turned and left.

Day after day she told people about her school. And day after day, she went to the trash piles behind the fancy hotels and to the dump near the school. She begged for empty boxes and crates. She found old pieces of wood, broken chairs, old cloth, and broken dishes.

She hauled these things back to the cabin and fixed them up. Cardboard boxes became desks for the children. Old orange crates became seats. An old packing crate became her desk. An old barrel turned upside down became her chair. Neighbors helped her scrub the floors, wash the windows, and paint the cabin inside and out.

After just a few weeks, the cabin was beginning to look like a school. But as the school took shape, Mrs. Bethune faced more problems. She had received just enough money from people to pay the first month's rent. Now she had to buy food and other supplies to keep the school going, but she had only one dollar left. What would she do? She wasn't sure, but she knew she'd find a way.

3

Pies and Songs
for a School

Mrs. Bethune thought about the men working on the railroad. She thought about some of the rich people in Daytona and the people staying at the fancy hotels. She wondered what she could do to get more money to run the school. Then an idea flashed into her mind.

Pies! she thought. She would make sweet potato pies and sell them to people. She began to figure out what she needed: pie pans and a pot to cook the potatoes in, flour and lard, eggs and sugar. These things would cost more than a dollar, but what she couldn't buy, she would borrow. She'd find a way.

Mrs. Warren loaned her flour and lard. Then Mrs. Bethune went to the grocery store and spent her last dollar on pie pans, a pot, eggs, sugar, and sweet potatoes. "Wrap every item separately, please," she told the store owner. When her school opened, the students would be able to use the paper to write on.

Now Mrs. Bethune had a way to make some extra money for the school. She began baking the pies, and they sold well. She had the extra money needed to open her school.

On October 4, 1904, Mrs. Bethune stood just inside the doorway of the cabin, which was now as neat and tidy as could be. Outside on the porch, five girls—Anne, Celeste, Lena, Lucille, and Ruth—aged eight to twelve, were waiting to enter the school. They were poor children. They had no shoes, and their clothes were full of patches. But they were happy to be going to school.

Mrs. Bethune rang a little bell and called each girl's name. As each one came through the doorway, Mrs. Bethune greeted her. "Good morning. I'm Mrs. Bethune. Please come in. We've been expecting you. I hope you will be happy with us."

After all the girls were at their box desks, Mrs. Bethune said a prayer. Then she led the girls and Albert in singing a song of faith.

Mrs. Bethune sat on her barrel chair behind her packing-box desk that had a bright cloth tied around it. She began giving the children their lessons. Instead of real pencils, they used burnt sticks of wood. For ink they used juice squeezed from berries. For pens they used feathers from geese and chickens. For paper they used the wrapping paper Mrs. Bethune got from the grocery store. They did not have books, but they began to learn anyway.

The students learned skills that would help them get jobs and take care of themselves when they were older. In addition to reading, writing, and arithmetic, they learned to memorize and recite poetry and to paint pictures. But they also learned to cook, to be neat, and to take care of their health. They learned to sew and to make brooms and rugs. They learned to fix broken dishes and furniture from the dump. At Mrs. Bethune's school, they learned things they couldn't learn anywhere else.

More and more parents began sending their daughters to Mrs. Bethune's school. But only a few could afford to pay the weekly fee. Mrs. Bethune made and sold more pies, and her students helped her. Still, as the school grew, so did its expenses. The sweet potato pies did not bring in enough money to buy all the supplies needed to keep the school open.

Mrs. Bethune began thinking of another way to raise money. She remembered how much she loved to sing. When she taught at Miss Laney's school, she sang in a chorus. The chorus sang at churches and homes around town. People paid money to hear

them, and the money helped Miss Laney run her school. Daytona Beach could use a good chorus, thought Mrs. Bethune. And her school could use the money.

The next day Mrs. Bethune announced to her students that they were going to start a chorus. She taught them many of the songs she knew. She even taught them a few songs she had learned as a girl from her own great-grandmother Sophia, who was the grand-daughter of a chief in West Africa.

Mrs. Bethune took the girls around to churches, hotels, and clubs in Daytona. Before they sang Mrs. Bethune told the audience about her school. Later she passed around an old hat, and people dropped coins into it to help the school.

Even more parents sent their daughters to Mrs. Bethune's school. By 1906 there were nearly 250 students. She could not turn any-one away, and classes in the cabin were get-ting very crowded. The school needed even more money and more space.

Mrs. Bethune found the space in an old barn behind the cabin. Mr. Williams was glad to let her rent it. But it needed to be fixed up, too. Once again neighbors and students helped out. Once again, Mrs. Bethune found a way.

4

A Swamp Becomes a School Ground

Mrs. Bethune had been so busy she hardly had time to think about the dream that was coming true. One day, however, she looked around at the cabin and the barn. She saw the students coming and going to classes, and she smiled proudly. She had begun a school for black girls, and it was working. But at the same time, she had to struggle each month to pay the bills.

Every month she had to pay Mr. Williams rent on the cabin. Suppose she bought some land. Then she wouldn't have to pay rent anymore. There was an idea! The land would be hers, and she could build a real school building just the way she wanted it.

She began looking around town for some property. Not far from the cabin, she found a large lot for sale. The lot was surrounded by tall oak trees. But beneath the giant moss-draped branches stood a swamp full of weeds and garbage. And the price! It was $250! But Mrs. Bethune didn't say anything. Instead, she looked carefully around the soggy ground.

As she gazed at the weeds and the garbage, the swamp began to disappear. In its place, a beautiful green lawn with beds of flowers stretched in the shade under the towering oak trees. In the center of the lawn stood a strong red-brick building—her new school. Mrs. Bethune smiled. She saw what the swamp could become, and she had an idea for a way to make it happen.

She went back to the school and talked to the parents, teachers, and children. She told them she was going to have an ice-cream party to raise money for a new school. Everyone in Daytona would be invited.

For days Mrs. Bethune, the students, teachers, and many parents worked hard. They made big batches of ice cream and hundreds of small pies. On the day of the party, people from all over Daytona came. They paid a penny for a slice of pie or for two big scoops of ice cream.

After the party Mrs. Bethune gathered up all the coins and tied them in her handkerchief. Then she went to Mr. Kinsey, the owner of the swamp land.

"What do you need for a down payment?" she asked.

"How much have you got?" asked Mr. Kinsey.

Mrs. Bethune opened her handkerchief and let five dollars in pennies, nickels, and dimes spill out on the table.

Mr. Kinsey stared at the coins for a moment. "Is that all you have?" he asked, frowning.

"It's all I have today, but I'll get the rest," Mrs. Bethune said confidently. "Just give me time, and I'll get the rest."

Mr. Kinsey thought about it, then looked at Mrs. Bethune carefully. A smile spread across his face. "Well," he said, "you've got an honest face. I guess you will."

Before Mr. Kinsey could say anything more, Mrs. Bethune thanked him and was gone. That afternoon she, her students, and several adults began clearing away the weeds and garbage from the land.

Some of the railroad workers helped drain the water from the swamp. After a few months, the land was dry and ready to be built on. But how would Mrs. Bethune build a building? Where would she get the money? Where would she find the builders?

5

A Real School at Last

At the old school, Mrs. Bethune began to give evening classes for the men and women of Daytona's black community. Some of the men worked for the railroad. Others were carpenters, plumbers, bricklayers, gardeners, and handymen. Skilled workers like these could help build a school, Mrs. Bethune thought. All she needed to do was to ask. And she did.

The workers were eager to help build her school, but they couldn't build the whole thing. Most days they worked at their jobs until dark. It was almost impossible to find

33

spare time in daylight to work on the school. Mrs. Bethune would still need to hire full-time builders. But her volunteer workers got the job started. Little by little, the adult students dug the earth and began laying bricks. They cut wood and put pipes in place. The walls of the school began to rise.

Mrs. Bethune and the younger students continued to raise money by singing. They also made more pies and sold more ice cream. But they were not able to bring in enough money to pay for all the sand, bricks, glass, pipes, and other materials needed for building the school. They didn't have enough to pay full-time builders.

Mrs. Bethune began to think of a way to get more money. There were a few very rich white people whose doorbells she had not rung yet. These were people from the North, such as Mr. James Gamble, who owned winter homes in Daytona Beach. She wondered if perhaps some of them would like to become trustees of the school—people who

would help her run the school. One breezy afternoon she rode her bicycle over to Mr. Gamble's big house.

"Are you the woman trying to build a school here?" he asked when she arrived at his door. Indeed she was, she announced. She told Mr. Gamble about her school. Then she invited him to visit the school anytime. She didn't ask for money. That could wait. First let him come and see for himself, she thought.

A few days later, Mr. Gamble showed up at the cabin. Everyone was busy making pies. Mrs. Bethune welcomed him and took him on a tour of the cabin and the barn. Mr. Gamble looked at the boxes and crates the children used as chairs and desks. He saw the burnt sticks they used for pencils. He saw the unfinished walls of the new building.

Mrs. Bethune's school did not look like any school Mr. Gamble had ever seen before. He looked worried and confused.

"Where is the school you told me about?" he asked her.

Her brown eyes twinkling, Mrs. Bethune smiled and folded her arms across her chest. "In my mind, in my spirit," she said proudly, placing one hand over her heart. "I'm asking you to be trustee of a glorious dream," she continued, "trustee of the hope I have in my heart for my people."

Mr. Gamble saw the hope shining in Mrs. Bethune's eyes. He also saw her determination. He knew she would build her school, no matter what.

So Mr. Gamble agreed to become a trustee. He agreed to meet with Mrs. Bethune and with other men and women to make decisions about the school. Together they would make sure the new school was built. They would make sure the school had money to educate Daytona's black children.

Then Mr. Gamble wrote out a check for $150 and handed it to Mrs. Bethune. When she saw how much the check was for, she smiled joyfully and shook his hand. It was the beginning of a good partnership.

By October 1907, workers had finished the roof over the new four-story school building. But the inside of the school still needed a lot of work. The floors were bare, and there weren't many windows in place. Mrs. Bethune decided to move the girls into the school anyway, and classes began.

She named the new building Faith Hall. Over the main door of the school she placed a sign that said ENTER TO LEARN. On the inside, she put another sign over the door that said DEPART TO SERVE.

Mrs. Bethune wanted her students to study hard and to use what they learned to help others. This is what she herself had done. With the help of many people—rich and poor, black and white—she built a school to serve her people. Later in her life she said, "Most people think I am a dreamer. . . . Through dreams many things have come true."

Epilogue

By 1914, just ten years after it first opened, Mrs. Bethune's school was a full-time high school. At that time there was only one other high school for black children in the whole state of Florida.

Across the road from the school, Mrs. Bethune bought more land and began a farm. The students took care of the farm and its animals. They ate some of the food they grew and sold the rest to raise money for the school. She wanted the school to be self-sufficient, like her students.

The young people who graduated from the

school were trained in cooking, nursing, homemaking, and teaching. They could get jobs, and they could help other people learn. Eventually the school joined with a school for boys and became Bethune-Cookman College. Mrs. Bethune was the first president of the college.

Mrs. Bethune died in 1955, but the school she began still exists today. Bethune-Cookman College has many large buildings on many acres of rich Florida land. About 2,300 young men and women attend the college every year.

Afterword

When Mary McLeod Bethune began working to build her school, she was not a famous person. Newspaper reporters and historians didn't follow her around and record everything she said and did. That came later after her school was established and she became a spokesperson for the rights of African Americans.

In retelling her story we had to rely on biographies and memories written many years after the early days of Mrs. Bethune's work. The words, thoughts, and actions described here are as they were remembered in these later accounts. All conversations shown in quotation marks are taken from these sources.

Notes

Page 3 Many southern states had what were called "Jim Crow laws." These laws stated that whites and African Americans could not use the same public places, such as parks, schools, drinking fountains, railroad cars, and even tele-

43

phone booths. These laws stayed in effect from about 1880 to the 1960s.

Pages 3–4 There were many elementary schools for black children scattered throughout the South. Most of them, however, had very little money for supplies and were open only three or four months of the year. In South Carolina in 1882, there were schools for blacks in nearly half of the state's counties. These schools were open only four months of the year. Mrs. Bethune's hometown, Mayesville, however, was in one of South Carolina's counties that had no schools for blacks until 1886.

Page 6 Mr. Bethune was not as excited about starting a school for blacks as Mrs. Bethune was. Even so, he encouraged her to go to Daytona to build her dream. As the school began to grow, Mr. Bethune realized Mrs. Bethune was devoting her life to helping other people. He felt she would not have time to be a wife and mother, too. He went back to South Carolina alone, where he died in 1919.

Page 11 Many African-American neighbor-hoods in the North and South were poor and run down like the Daytona Beach community. City and state governments simply spent more money on white communities than on black communities. For example, South Carolina spent $13.95 for every white child in a public school in 1915 and only $2.57 for each black child.

Page 11 Local and state governments did not help African Americans because African Americans were not allowed to vote in many communities and states. Southern states, in particular, kept blacks from voting with special rules and taxes designed by white politicians to exclude black voters. (No women—white or black—could vote at this time.)

The rules stated that for a man to vote, he had to pass a difficult reading and writing test, show that he owned property, or show that he paid taxes. This rule kept some poor white men from voting, too. So the politicians added a clause to the rule that required men to show proof that one of their relatives had been able to vote before January 1, 1867. No African-American men were allowed to vote in the South before that date, so none of their relatives from 1895 to 1910 could vote either. This clause became known as the "Grandfather Clause."

Page 16 Mrs. Bethune's school was not a public school. It was not run or paid for by the city of Daytona Beach or the state of Florida. Mrs. Bethune wanted it to be a private school so that she could control what the students learned. She believed that they should learn things they would not be taught in a public school, such as farming skills and dressmaking.

Page 23 Mrs. Bethune's son Albert was the only boy to attend her school when it opened. In 1908, he went to Atlanta, Georgia, to attend Miss Laney's school, which had begun to enroll boys.

Page 40 Even by 1916 there were only sixty-seven public high schools for African-American students in the United States. No more than 20,000 black students went to high school at that time. Most African-American pupils attended only the first four grades of elementary school.

Richard Kelso lives and works in New York City where he is a staff writer for Curriculum Concepts. Mr. Kelso has also written *Days of Courage* and *Walking for Freedom* for the *Stories of America*.